I'm a Mosasaurus

CHERRY LAKE PRESS

Published in the United States of America by Cherry Lake Publishing
Ann Arbor, Michigan
www.cherrylakepublishing.com

Reading Adviser: Marla Conn, MS, Ed., Literacy specialist, Read-Ability, Inc.
Content Adviser: Kierstin Rosenbach, Ph.D. Candidate, Vertebrate Paleontology, University of Michigan
Book Designer: Jennifer Wahi
Illustrator: Jeff Bane

Photo Credits: © MR1805/iStock.com, 5; © CoreyFord/iStock.com, 7; © Earth theater/Shutterstock.com, 9; © Victor Loki/Shutterstock.com, 11; © Rich Carey/Shutterstock.com, 13; © Dotted Yeti/Shutterstock.com, 15; © Sergey Orlov/Shutterstock.com, 17; © pick/Shutterstock.com, 19; © nicolasvoisin44/Shutterstock.com, 21; © K. Nakao/Shutterstock.com, 23; Cover, 2-3, 12, 20, 22, 24, Jeff Bane

Library of Congress Cataloging-in-Publication Data

Names: Nelson, Jake, author. | Bane, Jeff, 1957- illustrator.
Title: I'm a mosasaurus / Jake Nelson; illustrator, Jeff Bane.
Description: Ann Arbor, Michigan: Cherry Lake Publishing, [2021] | Series: My dinosaur adventure | Includes index. | Audience: Grades K-1
Identifiers: LCCN 2020002494 (print) | LCCN 2020002495 (ebook) | ISBN 9781534168534 (hardcover) | ISBN 9781534170216 (paperback) | ISBN 9781534172050 (pdf) | ISBN 9781534173897 (ebook)
Subjects: LCSH: Mosasaurus--Juvenile literature.
Classification: LCC QE862.S65 N45 2021 (print) | LCC QE862.S65 (ebook) | DDC 567.9/37--dc23
LC record available at https://lccn.loc.gov/2020002494
LC ebook record available at https://lccn.loc.gov/2020002495

Printed in the United States of America
Corporate Graphics

table of contents

About the author: Jake Nelson was born and raised in Minnesota, where he enjoys everything from watching the Twins at Target Field to strolling along the shore of Lake Superior. He writes books, blogs, and content for the web.

About the illustrator: Jeff Bane and his two business partners own a studio along the American River in Folsom, California, home of the 1849 Gold Rush. When Jeff's not sketching or illustrating for clients, he's either swimming or kayaking in the river to relax.

Hello! I'm a Mosasaurus.
I live in the water.

I lived 70 million years ago.

This was called the **Mesozoic era**.

I am about 50 feet (15 meters) long.

That is as large as a whale!

I am a **reptile**.

Most other reptiles live on land.

Why do you think some creatures like living in the water?

Reptiles do not have **gills** like fish. We cannot breathe underwater.

I like to stay close to the shore.

I swim to the **surface** to take a breath.

I can hold my breath for a long time.

Sometimes I dive to catch my **prey**.

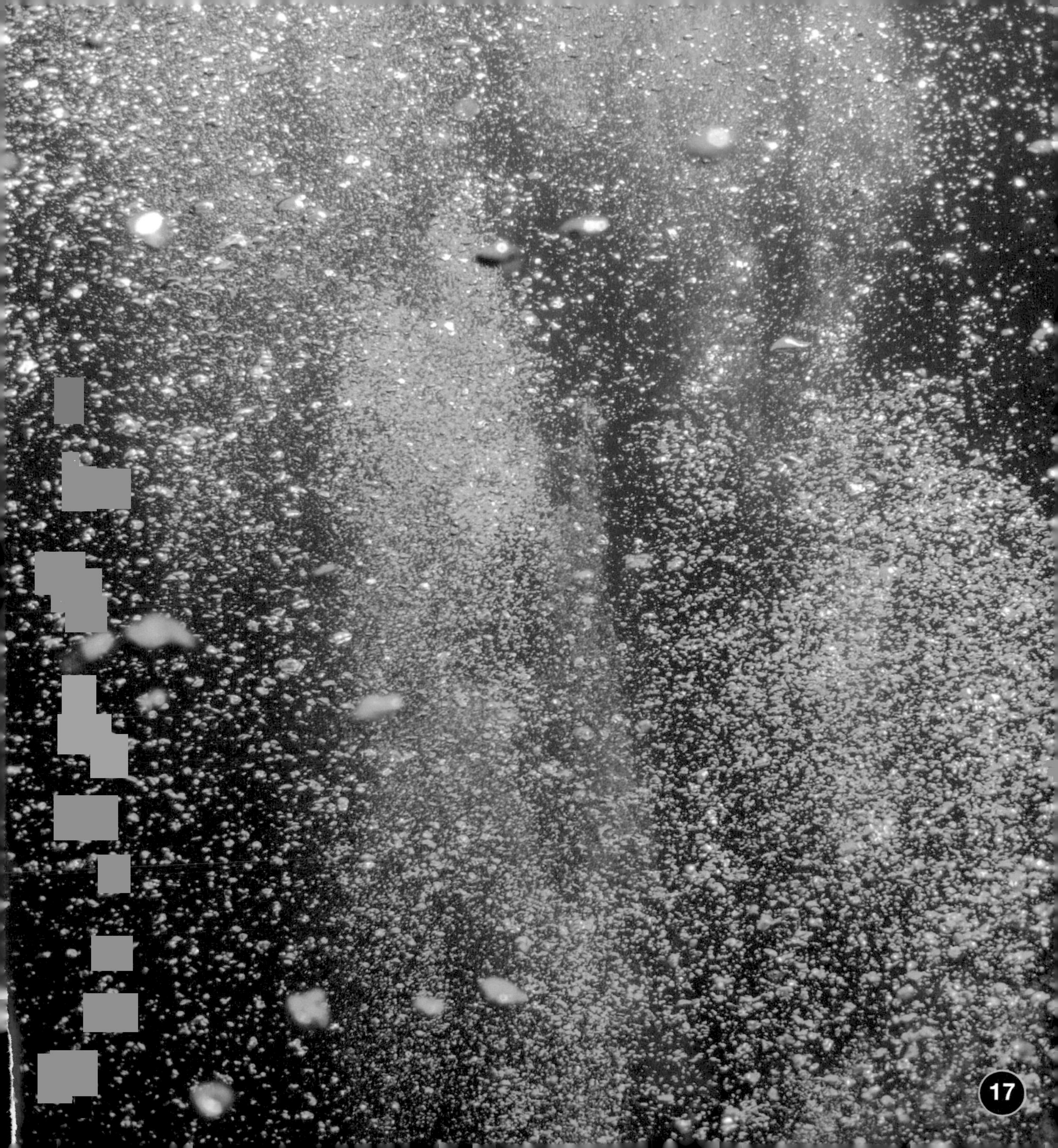

I'm a **carnivore**.

I'll eat anything that crosses my path.

What other sea creatures have a tail like this?

I have a large tail.

It helps **propel** me through the water.

Dinosaurs may have ruled the land.

But I ruled the water!

glossary

carnivore (KAHR-nuh-vor) a creature that only eats other living things, like animals or bugs

gills (GILZ) small openings on the side of a fish that allow them to breathe underwater

Mesozoic era (mez-uh-ZOH-ik ER-uh) the period of time when dinosaurs lived on Earth, between 245 million and 66 million years ago

prey (PRAY) a creature that is hunted by another creature

propel (pruh-PEL) to push something forward

reptile (REP-tye-uhl) a kind of animal with scaly skin, usually with a tail; lizards and snakes are reptiles

surface (SUR-fis) the top of the water

index